# Eating Apples

by

## Gail Saunders-Smith

# Pebble Books

an imprint of Capstone Press

# Pebble Books

Pebble Books are published by Capstone Press,
1710 Roe Crest Drive, North Mankato, Minnesota 56003.
www.capstonepub.com

*Library of Congress Cataloging-in-Publication Data*
Saunders-Smith, Gail.
    Eating Apples / by Gail Saunders-Smith.
    p. cm.—(Apples)
    Summary: Photographs and simple text describe different ways to enjoy
apples--whole, sliced, cooked, and juiced.
    ISBN-13: 978-1-56065-582-4 (hardcover)
    ISBN-10: 1-56065-582-8 (hardcover)
    ISBN-13: 978-1-56065-950-1 (softcover pbk.)
    ISBN-10: 1-56065-950-5 (softcover pbk.)
    1. Goats—Juvenile literature. [1. Goats.] I. Title. II. Series.
TX813.A6S28  1998
641.6'411—dc21                                                                97-29799

**Editorial Credits**

Lois Wallentine, editor; Timothy Halldin and James Franklin, design;
    Michelle L. Norstad, photo research

**Photo Credits**

Michelle Coughlan, 1, 4, 8, 12, 14
Unicorn Stock/Jean Higgins, cover; Paul A. Hein, 6; Doris
    Brookes, 10; David Cummings, 16; Pamela Pruett-Power, 18;
    Chuck Schmeiser, 20

Printed in China by Nordica.
0913/CA21301837
092013
007688R

# Table of Contents

4

apples

6

apple slices

apple   pie

apple   crisp

apple   sauce

apple  juice

apple cider

caramel apple

20

apple   fun

# Words to Know

**caramel**—a candy made from burnt sugar, butter, and milk; caramel is sometimes used to coat whole apples

**cider**—a drink made from pressed apples

**crisp**—a dessert made from fruit and a crumbled crust

**juice**—a drink made from the liquid of fruit or vegetables

**pie**—a dessert made from fruit and a pastry crust

**sauce**—fruit that is cooked until soft

# Read More

**Burckhardt, Ann L.** *Apples.* Mankato, Minn.: Bridgestone Books, 1996.

**Gibbons, Gail.** *The Seasons of Arnold's Apple Tree.* San Diego: Harcourt Brace Jovanovich, 1984.

**Micucci, Charles.** *The Life and Times of the Apple.* New York: Orchard Books, 1992.

# Internet Sites

Do you want to find out more about apples? Let FactHound, our fact-finding hound dog, do the research for you.

Here's how:

1) Visit *http://www.facthound.com*

2) Type in the **Book ID** number: **1560655828**

3) Click on **FETCH IT**.

FactHound will fetch Internet sites picked by our editors just for you!

## Note to Parents and Teachers

The Apple series supports national science standards on units on nutrition. This book describes and illustrates types of food made from apples. The photographs support early readers understanding of the text. The repetition of words and phrases helps early readers learn new words. This book also introduces early readers to subject-specific vocabulary words, which are defined in the Words to Know section. Early readers may need assistance to read some words and to use the Table of Contents, Words to Know, Read More, Internet Sites, and Index/Word list sections of the book.

## Index/Word List

**Word Count:** 17
**Early-Intervention Level:** 3